TERRACOTTA SMOKE

TERRACOTTA SMOKE

Poems by Toni Raben

Copyright © 2011 by Toni Raben.

Library of Congress Control Number: 2011900489
ISBN: Hardcover   978-1-4568-5153-8
             Softcover   978-1-4568-5152-1
             Ebook   978-1-4568-5154-5

All rights reserved. No part of this book may be reproduced or transmitted in any form or by any means, electronic or mechanical, including photocopying, recording, or by any information storage and retrieval system, without permission in writing from the copyright owner.

This book was printed in the United States of America.

To order additional copies of this book, contact:
Xlibris Corporation
1-888-795-4274
www.Xlibris.com
Orders@Xlibris.com
92521

The author gratefully acknowledges the following people for their support and encouragement:

>Riki and Howard Wagman
>Stephen Berg and the editors of American Poetry Review
>Steve Braunstein
>Henry Eckstein

CONTENTS

IMAGINED CRIMES

Ignorance, Ugliness, And Everything 13
Born At Night 14
Come To Life 15
Imagined Crimes 16
Visitation 19
I Told A Secret To The Wolves 21
She Never Looked As Good After That 22
The Darkness Is Deeper Now 25
The Texture Of No Light 27
Private Speak 28

JUST ONE OF THE GIRLS

Her Own Invention 33
Concubines 34
Flesh 35
Multiplication 36
Someone Else's Life 37
Pyramid 38
It Looked Like Life 39
Just One Of The Girls 40
Terracotta Smoke 42

UNLIT, UNSEEN

It's Too Early 47
The End Of Words 48
Unlit, Unseen 49
The End Of Quiet 50
The Meaning Of Echoes 51
Faith 52
Summarized 53

DNA

The Order 57
Luminosity 58
The Bed In Her Eyes 59
Divine Selection 60
Against Gravity 61
Her Mother 62

VANISHING

The End Of Her Eyes 65
Vanishing 66
A Smashed Vase 67
Invisibly Missed 68
Wait For Sleep 69

HER OCEAN

To My Mother 73
The Ladies On The Sand 75
The Essence Of Infinity 76
Paint Away The Ocean 77
The Stillness Of The Harbor 78
Her Ocean 79
Someone Opens Her Letter 80
ChlorIne Dream 81
I've Lost Time 82
Water's Edge 83
Whirling 84
She Pretends 85
My Father 87
Lullaby 88

CHEAP FINISH

Cold 91
Cheap Finish 92
Square One 93
Her Thoughts Found Me 94
Whoever Lives Wins 95
No Ears, No Lies 96
Lies Lived 97

INHALING LILACS

Shadows Became Jewels 101
Inhaling Lilacs 102
The Outline Of My Body 103
Psalms 104
Unsaid Words 105
Red Glass Vase 106
"No Poems" 107

BLIND SMOKE

Blind Smoke	111
9/11	112
When I Have Said Goodbye	113
Weep With Me	114

FAIRY TALES

Atoms Speaking	117
The Magic-Maker	118
In The Darkness	119
Monet Understood	120
Planting Flowers	121
Dear Wind	122
In Shadow	123
The Three Witches	124
Doorways	125
Wherever I Looked	126
Butterfly	127
Dharma	128
Eggplant	129
How Dare They	130
I Am A Colored Girl	131
Who Was I Kidding	132
Solid And Forever	133

IMAGINED CRIMES

IGNORANCE, UGLINESS, AND EVERYTHING

Ignorance
disguises itself
as austerity and piety
and always has
since the first person glowed
and the second person
wished they could shine
and thought the glow
was the thing
and not the invisible
unseen heart

And ugliness
disguises itself
as beauty
and age becomes a child
and until you can know
the pure heart of yourself
you can't know
the truth of another

Everything
is shaken and shined
and cleansed
and always has been
since the first person
mistakenly thought
they had sinned

*Published in *The American Poetry Review* November/December 2003 as # *12*

BORN AT NIGHT

The records of myself
connected to my father
that live in the ether
between heaven and earth
in a black-and-white picture
have been destroyed

Jealousy was tempting
and cold
and born at night

She had cut out the memories
and put away the meanings
of an innocent moment
that confused her

The mirror had been her mother
the camera her lover

The stolen images would
reappear in colors
careful to be quiet
and not awaken jealousy
stealing back the cutout memories
of our secret signs
and purity

We dug our feet
into the cool damp sand

COME TO LIFE

Out the door
she was cloaked in gin
out the other
I could hear her scream
as I fled with the flowers
she dug her nails in my dreams

I was the far and the few between
a doll come to life
I was the promise
the way and the means

I was concealed
stripped of my shield
I had hidden my virtue
I was caught in her schemes

I was the paramour of innocence
I was tangled in today
my batteries were running out
and my Bible wouldn't pray

IMAGINED CRIMES

The sun
could see her heart
in the morning
before the residue
of paints would emulsify
and the goodness
of the little goddess
would be lost
for as long as the sun
would stay awake

She pleaded
without anyone knowing
to be seen
as the goddess of goodness
though
they wanted to keep her in the kitchen
doing the laundry

She would have to become
more profound
to change their perception
and for anyone to agree
to allow her
to keep on living

Writing letters to angels
a common laid plan
worked for a while
but needed follow-through

Resplendent beings
carried her to a holy saint
who helped her
get the proper footing
on a more ecstatic state

Grace like this
never comes
without introspection
which could keep you
in the kitchen
waiting to be transferred
to your next location

Location, location
not a vacation
an easy diversion
trading frequent miles
gaining temporary relief
from trying
to be known
as a much
better person

The happy sun
was looming behind the clouds
covering the dark city

She was trying to remember
when the saint had intervened
knowing that he had seen
the painting of her life
and the remnants of her suffering
the purity of her heart
he was always there
from the beginning

Did he want her to speak out?
or hide behind parallel truths
tip-toeing past her youth
agreeing to be born
at a later time
when she could understand
the perfection of her affliction
deciphering and decoding
the love
stitched and painted
through her life
of imagined crimes

VISITATION

They wanted her childhood to end
though she revisits it
in the still silence of morning

Opening a door
to a place
where her youth
had been appeased
and a bed
made only for her
with love
planted
disguised as flowers
keeping her safe and adored
before the night could reach her

They did not know
she was in danger
of losing the protection
and devotion
of the flowers

And the garden
she dreamed about
could fade
in the sun's
lost memory of morning

They wanted her to wake up
from the dream
of the visitation
of the angels
who cradled her
in their arms

Covering her
with love disguised
as platinum thread
wrapped all around
the pieces of her heart
that would break
without their adornment

I TOLD A SECRET TO THE WOLVES

I told a secret
and the wolves
fought over it

My heart bled
and fertilized
the ground

Flowers grew
with more secrets

Lovers put balm
on the wounds

Angels crossed-dressed as people
and were larger than humans
in six-inch heels

Celestial and genderless
floating and cradling
holding me
just above the ocean's surface
in a never ending
baptismal conclusion

SHE NEVER LOOKED AS GOOD AFTER THAT

I returned from somewhere
no one knew where
all of my children
their porcelain faces
the sticky hair
from gold to brown
to red
Revlon
my precious
and baby dear
my first real newborn
who needed my embrace
to live

We had a view
of a bridge
no one was really
part of our world
my children
mine

Today I returned
from somewhere
and all of my girls
were gone
no one knew where
too stunned to speak
the shelves were stark
with no faces
only the pattern
on ceiling plaster
of prickly stucco
that would be terrible
if I fell upward

But now I'm seeing
empty shelves
someone is getting
some satisfaction
from this
somewhere

I don't know where she is
maybe in the other room
I had no more babies
no certainty
I deserved having my children taken

But I was a little girl
Ms. Revlon may have left
because of a bad shampoo
I tried

She never looked as good after that
maybe she was afraid
of what I might do next
I was such a bad mother
I should have taken better care
maybe the movie about the evil dolls
who talked while you slept
maybe I had made them bad
and someone found out
and
I deserve to have my babies
taken away
maybe I was too old at seven or so
maybe it was time
to let my babies go

One day not long after
somewhere
I found my babies strewn upon
someone's attic floor

*Published in *The American Poetry Review* November/December 2003 as # *9*

THE DARKNESS IS DEEPER NOW

Acquaintances
who once were friends
are angry because
you have gone away

He enters your dream
like Vanilla Haagen-Dazs
reading a Bible
reminding you of an interesting youth
you enjoyed spending

The darkness is deeper now
more than imagined
it glistens
and shivers
it is not a fairy tale
it is real
and can kill

Vanilla Haagen-Dazs
knows her better
she had served him her essence
as only a fool can
and drawn beauty
from clarified passion
turning her love to destruction
and back again

The night whispers in her ear
what it always meant to say

She sucks on the air
like the saints too pure to eat
her robes billowing
as she walks away
people bow down before her
and stay kneeling
when she is gone
and she holds a cross
and a star
and a Hindu linga
and dreams of burgers
and fries
and saving mankind

She finds her gaze in
the eyes of the
sacred seven
and stands alone
before the slayer and the slain
and then finds God
and turns her back
on heaven *

*Inspired by *Brahma* by Ralph Waldo Emerson

THE TEXTURE OF NO LIGHT

He's seen what toll a lack of love
can leave on the mirror's reflection

A sleeping self hears nothing
but dead voices

Resurrection is always a miracle
but can't be relied upon
and timing is everything
but it's best not to expect it

The radiant child lives quietly in the dark
and feels the texture of no light

Emerging without being alive
she bows down to a false image
that is the wicked girl they said she had become

Moving fearlessly into the reflected glass
God spoke
she awoke
asking for a diet coke

She could easily blend in as a live girl
who on a perfect day
could be seen floating among the lilies
in a mystical Monet

PRIVATE SPEAK

Whose joy
will she enter today
before breath
and the Times
has started
someone's life?

She jogs in her mind
next to greatness
where creatures
too familiar
dream by

She can be found
inventing a language
waiting to be heard

And private speak
understood by
two or three
their foreheads
carefully kissed
and pressed
before letting them leave

Inside her eyes
are widened

She sees the girl from Radcliff
who entered a world
of expectation

Peering over the fence
in Wuthering Heights
she is Heathcliff and Kathy
remembering
it's only a movie
and anything is possible
in New York

JUST ONE OF THE GIRLS

HER OWN INVENTION

Gazing into geisha eyes
locked behind ivory carved lotus gates
when family had to be forgotten
traded for truth
blurred by vermouth
and lost youth was a matter of opinion

Sure of her assets
she was her own invention
cruelty began before she walked in
the story told itself
with glazed over egg tempera
that time chipped away

She hoped her mask would be missed
no one who loved her
separated admiration from fiction

CONCUBINES

They were concubines
women of diplomacy
wives of the new millennium
elegant and crisp
magnificent painted faces

One constructed a bed of tears
the other wondered
what her youth was really worth

No one ever told the truth
and so I was going to be lonely
for the next thousand years

Art was the only metaphor for life
and metaphors were neither art
nor truth
nor part of life

Everyone is geisha

FLESH

She found herself caught
between life
and the glistening black death
which was beauty

She held on to the perfect mask
so desperately
it made her look like a crow
devouring its own carcass

We are all walking
in a pitch night
dead souls
looking for our mothers
to take us to a place
where beauty can't be seen
and no one trades on flesh

*Published in *The American Poetry Review* November/December 2003 as # *43*

MULTIPLICATION

Her soul
enfolded
in the shell
air chipping away
at hardened crystal
exposing dazzling treasure

She sent her vibrations out
to other worlds
enclosed in angelic feathers

She fell to her knees
invoking the avatars of old
Krishna, Buddha, Christ
she asks, "Does Barbie have a soul?
and
if not
why is she so adored?
and why does she multiply
at such an alarming rate?"

SOMEONE ELSE'S LIFE

The crows
picked away at the flesh
while little was left to love
and only he could find
the girl he had married

The mirrors around her cage
were taught to lie

Her mind accidentally wandered
into someone else's life

It was very fulfilling
until they asked her to leave

PYRAMID

Pyramid
crushed skull
pointed head
for beauty soul
pain and class
be thy rule

Feet of Geisha
wealthy wife
bound for dainty
crippled life

Pull the eyelids
up and back
never let them see you slack

Hide the evidence of
what you think
sans the nonessential blink
erase all trace of who you are
tucked behind a tiny scar

IT LOOKED LIKE LIFE

It looked like life
to the eye

Beauty ran screaming
and was horrified
at the thought of death

She was dressed up to look
like she was made from atoms
like the rest of us
breathing prana into a balloon
not expecting it to pop

Come and gone without a reason
for vanity to stay alive

The soul's night comes
to turn the TV off
when you have fallen asleep

JUST ONE OF THE GIRLS

They thought she was their saint
With her glistening hair
And her perfect feet
That chose to walk on sand

She could sell what they
Were looking for
With just the power of her eyes
And dream what they were dreaming
And make them love her
On command

Night falls
Morning arrives
In an unsolvable random equation

It seemed like any other day
Although her disciples were scarce
And no one was offering
Homage or oblation

She would have to get used
To the absence of chant
And be the kind of saint
Who did some things
She didn't like
And try it off the cuff
With no power in her eyes
Or at least it was disguised
As an uninvited stare

She didn't want to be
Just one of the girls
It would be hard
To cash out her style

She'd rather be
Like Elvis
Or Monroe
And leave them
Standing in the aisles

Much to her chagrin
She found the worship of her soul
Had to conform to the beauty
Of the body it lived in

As she was getting old
Or rather fully fading
Sympathy walked out
Her glow was not glowing
There was nothing left for trading

TERRACOTTA SMOKE

I should be hiding
in the morning magic
behind ideas
that need to be styled
and sewn
and dry-cleaned
translated into something
that can be discerned
by someone who may be
blind to innocence
or who could easily walk
over my body
on the dusty road
to be blown into the
mouth of the Ganges
where sacred cows
would hopefully
know me

I wonder if they can see
true beauty?
it's not dusted and clean
it sparkles
and changes
and morphs
into a transparent illusion
and is mostly unrecognizable

At the end of the road there is a brutal tug-of-war

The dust rises
and is displaced
on the steps
down to the funeral ghat
wild monkeys dance
while I sleep
or I'm awake
wondering
how many mornings
will be filled with
cows
climbing over
breathless bodies
puffed in
terracotta smoke
recently
unoccupied

UNLIT, UNSEEN

IT'S TOO EARLY

When you have forgotten
why anyone knows you
under a night
that sticks to your soul
like tar on fine blonde hair
with less hope
and more despair
than falling
or sinking
or jumping out of

Someone grabs you by the collar
when you were hoping it's not real
and says you're not going anywhere

And for as long as the night
has enough lack
to stave off light
your voice will whisper to the walls
and be absorbed by
no one hearing

And in the day
sitting in a cafe
looking like
a brilliant bouquet
and amazed at
the wonder of the sun
and coffee
and
it's too early
to start
counting

Counting backwards

THE END OF WORDS

Last night
sound left

Pulling tissue paper
out of an empty gun

Last night at the end of words
spiders wove their opinions
into the wrong intentions

Last night
of panic
when all the doors are closed
and the lights go out
just when everyone should stay
everyone leaves
and the darkness
shaves off its mouth

*Published in *The American Poetry Review* November/December 2003 as # *19*

UNLIT, UNSEEN

Torn pieces
of nightfall
fly
before the sky
becomes its darkest

Expecting it
to arrive on its toes
perspective changes
when at first the blackness glows
and sews itself
to your unseen body
so tightly
it may never release you

Everything is fine
while you are still floating
avoiding the ground

As the first hint
of dawn approaches
and the unlit tomb
that seemed to swallow you whole
has decided to let you go
someone hits high speed rewind
and arrives with the sun
if you can just make it till morning
when the darkness does not own you

THE END OF QUIET

Within the inside pitch

When night is at
the end of quiet

She speaks
to silent poets
and listens
for slight fluctuations
in the heartbeats
of naked soldiers

Their random words
pour
into
the
emptiness
of her soul

With no way
to understand
the loneliness
of an invisible universe

Colors
cross over
and she hopes
someone will hear

THE MEANING OF ECHOES

She walked through the house
sealing winter out

As each door closed
she heard the echo
of those who came before

Poets were the very few
most froze before they knew
their words
had any meaning

Sometimes they were silenced
after they were overheard
speaking to God
in the first
faint
memory of morning

FAITH

Getting used to
getting used to
slipping from the ship
swallowing words
hold on to the page

The invisible invisible
reaches out
as it watches land fade
talking to nothing
casting my words upon the water

believing
believing
believing

SUMMARIZED

Her words are pinned
to the executioner's bed

She lies to sleep

Memory and heart
rinsed and bleached
waking to the echoes
of syllable and sound
removed and summarized

Her critics would not stop looking
to see what was missing
inside her frozen winter eyes

DNA

THE ORDER

She was weaving holy passages

The waiter used a small crumb device
to pick up her tears

She was inventing computer codes
an indirect and circumspect
network of possibilities

Only genius was intrigued by her mind

She called out in the night
equipped with a collision avoidance system
she moved the ocean
a juxtaposition of divine order

Remembering a commercial of an egg
"This is your heart frying on the pavement"

Later in the evening
she looked for signs
of a frictionless flow
and wondered if the waiter
had understood the order

LUMINOSITY

Everything had been written
before
and woven into blonde hair
draped over someone's
idea of a luminous mind

You may hold on
you may let go
he thinks
a glowing inferno

His calmness
makes you feel small
like someone who's afraid
to renew their passport

You are thinking
of closing your eyes
while he writes his sonnets
by breathing

His thoughts can be felt
by leaning down
and gently touching
his mouth

THE BED IN HER EYES

Her mother was
permanently fixed
hypnotically
peeking out
from the warm pools of light
within her daughter's eyes

It was the enunciation
smack dab
on Mary's face
not of alabaster
but tinted with honey
with ways and powers
and hidden gifts
from a far-off culture

Anyone could see
her mother had made
a bed in her eyes
and would be passing
secrets of seduction
of matter and flesh
down through her DNA
with little plans for leaving

Inheritance had its price
the leftover life of a missing gene
that her son-in-law
would spend the rest of his
memory grieving

DIVINE SELECTION

In slow motion
in reverse direction
fragments of broken glass
shattered back together
catching the anger and the sadness
on film

The guarantee of resurrection
and divine selection
promise to redeem her fears
and reason for not waking

Without the knowledge of her name
she would look the same
her life was still untitled
she stopped answering the phone
and then she stopped breathing

AGAINST GRAVITY

He wore a fiber
of purest gold
and floated against
the gravity
of ignorance

Magnetized
by the pull
of permanent
innocence

A marionette
let go
I fell to my knees
he had decorated
my heart with flowers
and taken refuge
in my destiny

My purity
was authenticated
he whispered

HER MOTHER

It was her mother,
she had to disappear
her words became smaller
her life was getting closer to the air

"What a pair" she whispered
through empty tin cans
"I love you" her mother spoke too

It was hard to explain,
the likelihood of being here
in the way
her mother pictured,
was slim,
or maybe the same

Time was the trickster
or the messenger
we didn't understand
rendering everything
sooner than later

The future was left in life's wake
the train had sped up
now was the time to hurry and live
and plan

Her mother would be there
when she arrived
it would be worth the deception
and the disguise
to not have known
her child was ill

VANISHING

THE END OF HER EYES

I searched through the tunnel
at the end of her eyes
and heard the sounds
of a music-less place
where she lived alone
with a portrait that never changed
though she had prayed
that it would repaint itself
every morning early
though hope would end at night

No dreams could swim
to rescue her
from the waterless moat
that was the place
she lived alone
that was her home
where she had once remembered
the meaning of a miracle

VANISHING

She was the only one
in love forever
sitting in uncommon simplicity
among the roses

Who was the woman
with the vanishing child?
Who will see her in their garden?
Who will ask them for tea
and kiss the boy's silent mouth?

Or fear
it will pull them
into a night
that will end without morning

*Published in *The American Poetry Review* November/December 2003 as # *27*

A SMASHED VASE

A smashed Vase

They forced her to swallow a fragment
No one had the right to interfere with hope
She spoke into the clear air

Her voice cut through a black night
turning green into morning

She was not certain
that heaven would return from work

The doctor said
a thousand swans
had left her body
sometime before dawn

INVISIBLY MISSED

A child lived in silence
talking to bodies
that could not see her
wandering
through a forgotten time
waking up
in a white and plain country church
holding on
to her mother's skirts
surrounded by
politely sad people

She was invisibly missed
on a glistening
fresh cut
green grass day

Soon everyone would leave
to eat lovely things
she would have to let go
of her mother's skirt
and try to remember

She would have to have a lovely lunch
somewhere else
some other time
on some other day

WAIT FOR SLEEP

My angel writes for me
with the TV on
she waits for me to wake
she prays for me
catching butterflies
between commercials
she's wise

A giant woman
looms while I sleep

My angel takes my mind
back to the range
where Roy Rogers was
before he met Dale

And even Dale was OK
I'm sure she was kind
and Trigger was good
so good
like my angel
I bet

If you listen to my angel from here
my voice should get louder
than the TV

I don't have the courage
to wait for sleep

HER OCEAN

TO MY MOTHER

We found our love
on an unconditional beach
and watched the water
you arranged
rise and fall

And you wished that you could sing
I composed you a song
we painted on the sand
I brushed your pretty hair
afternoons were meant for shopping
all the seashells we could stand
We dreamed we were together
placing secrets in our hands

We would awaken to the sound
of our own bells
digging deep within our hearts
there were stories we could tell

Our beauty was confirmed
in the reflection in our eyes
beauty is the truth
and lack of truth is just a lie

Never ask what someone sees
who is not grounded in your soul
they are merely dying cameras
whose lenses have grown old

They say there is no end to love
no night
nor light of day
no life in what is said out loud
no debt that's left to pay

We are the paint that
makes the painting
not the mind
and not the hand
we are the very stuff of life
together on the sand

                                                  Your loving daughter,
                                                  Toni

THE LADIES ON THE SAND

The ladies on the sand
suspended by familiarity
touched by steel blue clouds
creamy songs pierced through their dream of rain
or had it once been
and not again
would it be permanently dry
in the weather of this painting
an innocent afternoon
from which the girls had never returned

Perhaps they never left
the artist's studio

Had he only wished to place them by the sea
and their posture and expression
could never be
under a steel blue cloud

They never gave their permission

THE ESSENCE OF INFINITY

The painted ocean splashed a clear glaze
polishing those souls past and future
stones placed on my table

Vividly connecting
the essence of infinity
to a kingdom on view

Water surrounded by mountains
a sacred life
a universe
in the color of Yves Klein Bleu

Pavarotti
Pyramid
Pieta
gently put them down
I found them on the beach
contained in glowing sound
their sparkling lineage
impeccably concealed

They are the knower and the known
their silent tone
revealed

PAINT AWAY THE OCEAN

Paint away the ocean
I cannot paint what is written

I lie at the shore
among rocks and seashells
reborn each morning
I travel through the ancient ether
long before you have thought about
a cup of coffee

Listening to the trivial
and seeing the complex
the teller mistakes love for similarity

I belong to the source of everything
I rise and fall to the occasion
in a gold encrusted castle
surrounded by a moat filled with tears
lending my heart for the evening

Quick-witted humor
informs the listener
that I am more than a leaf

Pulling the rice paper fan
over my face
quickly disappearing
before anyone can see
that I am a leaf
and nothing is more

THE STILLNESS OF THE HARBOR

The boat pushed
away
leaving the shore
with no provisions
for a welcome home

She was often mistaken
for the stillness of the harbor

No one cared about
the beginning of a moment
or divine conception
or noticed it leaving

With the speed of courage
she found faces
she had walked by
whose eyes could have been
traced over her own

Looking back
into a glass
holding letters
written in a floral pattern
filled with water
and people she's forgotten

HER OCEAN

A shock of feelings
that look like flowers

Melodious words
erase the past

Leaving her alone
on a beach

Hearing emotions
turn back into words
through the sound
of a curling wave

Her ocean is translating
a message
from her stillness

No one is asking
about the magic
that surrounds her
afraid of what
she may say

Each one looking
for a raised platform
so they can seem taller
and the truth
appear smaller

SOMEONE OPENS HER LETTER

Someone opens her letter

The completed words
woven together on a page
mailed to the sailor
who is always waiting
to be set free
inspired by the hope
of an end to his longing

She is the captain
who promises daylight
and a meaning to his journey

Or would he wish for the simple
whiteness of a tree
that has been begged and pounded
out of desperation
and finally gives up what
was once its strength

to allow her to imprint the words clearly
on the life that has been
sacrificed
and may never find the sailor
or the
ocean

CHLORINE DREAM

The painter gazed into the blueness
of his chlorine dream

Moving currents by desire
causing undulating patterns
of turquoise water
pulling the viewer out to sea

Concealing the identity
of his partially submerged
imaginary lover

Seeing a new canvas
wanting to start over
he wondered
how long love can stay alive
without breathing

I'VE LOST TIME

I wondered this morning
and wandered through rooms
flowers filling my vision
crowding out empty spots

Boats glide below
I look away
I've lost time
now what's left
is froth like snow

And the Times is saying
"The secret of happy nuns
who live quite long
may be found on their faces"
Looking into their eyes
finding black and white snapshots
from simple box cameras
or prying Hasselblads
exposing details
some would rather not

A photo trail to see
when the gleam was still there
and in those who die young
when was innocence
replaced by fear

WATER'S EDGE

She started to sing
at water's edge
in the cool fluorescent glow
of white dress
someone had washed it with red

Trying to cleanse their soul
passing the gene
to the next generation

She continued to sing
at water's edge
and begged the Gods
to come for lunch
and feed her the love
that had left the table
removing the evidence
and the suspicion
that could lead to the dress
one of too many clues
she would
need to forget

WHIRLING

I am a speedball
whirling crazily into the ocean
I am its aftermath
music and words have taken over
flying with song

I am a beautiful boat
with no names for its passengers

I am too tired to speak
arguing with myself for no reason
I am unimaginable sweetness
I am too finite to notice
when sound is gone

My face rose over
the gray pastel ocean

The sun swam inside my body
talking to cells who remember
within the walls that protect
the love I have shared
with whoever passed by

SHE PRETENDS

She pretends to be empowered
While your senses are enlivened
You imbibe her with a dream
She awakens you to colors
A mirage out of your window
Stars are dotted in the landscape
You're too wise to fall asleep
And for a moment beauty whispers
You are all alone

You are counting times remembered
From a voice whose song is softer
And the clouds that you could count on
Moving quickly past your future
Now have stayed too long

And the ones you had considered
And the life that you have tasted
And the truth that was not spoken
And the gifts that you have wasted
Are all coming home

The ocean saves your secrets
And the river is your lover
And you wait for your directions
And the sky lets you discover
That you're not alone

There are those around you
And they do not look familiar
You're relieved to know they found you
Drifting on the mighty river
And the sails are gone

And you imbibe her with a dream
And she awakens you to colors
And for a fleeting moment
You're together on the river
You are coming Home

MY FATHER

When my father came back to me
from the memory of the silent ocean
and the fishing boat held stories
I was too young to understand
we sat on the sand
his sorrow rolled out to sea
losing myself in the white breakers
everything went away
the first man I loved
came back to me
he would stay awake
through my sleep
and keep a place that is safe
for a fisher girl

LULLABY

Lie down
go to sleep
little one
I'll blow roses on your feet
don't cry
no one can see through your eyes
the glass window is not there
don't cry
don't have a care
sleep on
don't cry
don't have a care
sleep on

The wind will braid your hair
tangle us in prayer
be listened to forever
when there's no mother there
sleep on
beauty one
child who's gone
where have you gone

CHEAP FINISH

COLD

The fingers
encircling the cola cup
signed out a language
on the cold sweat
of its paper sides

The outline
of what used to be his life
had congealed
with the clammy
watered down whispers
of the once sacrosanct

Someone unexpected
would feel the message
beneath the rumors

She was not put off
by the idea of deception
She was practical
and knew that love
cannot be stolen

The supposedly holy
were really just bitter
at not being the one
he had chosen
to leave with

CHEAP FINISH

Her heart felt like a blade
he could not tell
steel from platinum

For a while his wealth
would be enough
to keep the knife at a safe distance

They had soldered their souls together
before he realized
the surface was not as fine
as he had hoped
and was actually quite dull

His dreams of pouring
a precious and malleable alloy
into a magnificent vessel
faded away
with the cheap finish
that eroded his false idea of love

SQUARE ONE

She tried to scrub him
off her skin
and was repulsed
to the core

She was convinced
that she was compassionate
but only to the point
of entering the ring

Then
when he clammed up
and got lost
she thought his family
could have him back
she was finished
and closing up shop

HER THOUGHTS FOUND ME

Her thoughts found me
like chalk on a blackboard
she was weeping and didn't know
she was almost drowning

When her mouth
was slightly above water
I told her to look in my eyes
I had painted a beautiful picture
if I could make her believe
it could actually be her

My picture was not perfect enough
for her tears to stop
although she acknowledged
that she belonged to a superior life
alone somewhere
with some handsome millionaire
who
of course
was never there

She continued to live in hope
of someone pulling her out
I said she needed to get word
to the little girl
who got the wrong message
that made her believe
that what's true is not
and that love looks perfect on the outside
and is never blurred
by the tears of almost drowning

WHOEVER LIVES WINS

Whoever lives wins
as she folded his clothes
in the drawer
or so it appeared
to the almost departed

Picasso was the only one
left standing on the tarmac
gazing upward
at a Titian sky

Knowing the answers were sealed
and the balance of what was given
stolen and revealed
could be on the bottom
of a glazed
unrippled lake
or in a morsel
of an oversized
overpriced
pompously buttered
scone at brunch

NO EARS, NO LIES

Although martyrdom
seemed like a bad idea
it was the only thing
that worked

Pure love
was always
the answer

It has no eyes
no ears
no lies
and lives
in the moment
and dies
in the illusion
that it has not been seen

And the message
on the machine
is always
the same

*Published in *The American Poetry Review* November/December 2003 as # *32*

LIES LIVED

The paper said
lies lived
but they don't

They spill onto the dream-colored carpet
and soak up the sin of it all

But they don't

Innocent feet press over the spot
that looks like new
and everyone forgot
what could have been
when the truth came through

They wash their fingerprints
off the walls
and tear up the floors
forgetting why the colors
could never look right
white was never
perfect white
Carpet
birch
marble
pine

Ripping up
and laying down
could never cover up
the lie

INHALING LILACS

SHADOWS BECAME JEWELS

Shadows became jewels
without the slightest provocation
reflecting thoughts of smoky quartz
believing atoms heard her voice
in a myriad of lights
in the middle of the night
bathed in glitter and Chopin

She placed the diamonds in her hand
talking to the woman soul
the wisdom ones from long ago
worshipped now for what they know

INHALING LILACS

Someone
is breathing
into the air
inhaling lilacs

I steal the first touch
of a soundless hum
that brushes past my cheek
softer than the dream
that won't let you leave

And you're stunned by your own sweetness
which you decide to keep a secret
and the morning's spilling over
like an alcoholic's gin
while you hide under the covers
with a cat instead of lovers
and you spend all of the day
licking honey off your skin

*Published in *The American Poetry Review* November/December 2003 as # *5*

THE OUTLINE OF MY BODY

I'm hiding at my table
trying to earn the truth
to justify the suicides
of other opened eyes
who cried over a baby blanket
too unraveled
that accidentally lost its form
in an old washing machine

I think the dead
are on my side
feeding me lines
with chocolate everything
my first party of the morning
chocolate and caffeine
I could have taught them
how to live

Inviting me to a dinner party
for the history
of the outline of my body
asking me to lie
in the hollow mold
and when it is time
they are there
they are there
my teachers
each one knows

*Published in *The American Poetry Review* November/December 2003 as # *24*

PSALMS

She traded stones
for carefully crafted days
by artists whose visions
resembled her own

How many stones remained
ringing in and ringing out
never knowing which
would awaken the end

A visit to Van Gogh or
taking a chance on a Vegas slot

She took the hard news
sitting down
facing her face
the one she most admired
softly cupping her cheeks
in the roundness of her palms
left to adore herself alone
waking from the end
of a life spent
reading psalms on the phone

UNSAID WORDS

Her unsaid words
filled up the clouds
that drifted past
the heart of hell
and acrobatic clowns rolled by
and tumbled on the ceiling
posing for the hands of God
their fingers never touching

They waited for the Sistine bells
so they could break for lunch

RED GLASS VASE

It looked like she
had lived her life
with the strain of blood
spilled in her house

It was a trick
played by the sun
shining through
a red glass vase
more complex
was the bouncing
of light
from its reflection
kissing the current
quickly shimmering
alive with desire
and dead without it

Happy to leave the confinement
of a fictional life
she was at least three people
at last count
but not
in the traditional sense
so many lived inside
and after God and saints
agreed to intervene
they chose the quiet loving one
to be their conscience
and their guide

"NO POEMS"

Words dispersed
in the air
through my window
that said
"no poems"

I kneeled down
to massage the feet
of whoever I hoped
to hear

Placing my lips
on their toes
offering
though not knowing
what I was giving

Chocolate-coated
candy hearts
melted between
the phone and my ear
nothing left for me there

Ice could disappear and leave
some life sustaining coolness
or it may reappear
and you may never see it

BLIND SMOKE

BLIND SMOKE

Where is my heart?
feeling for life in the dark

It was a perfect day
my husband looked up
and could see
the burning towers
he turned and walked
in my direction

I sat in what I believed
until today
was my perfect city view
friends called
from other places
glad we were safe

Emblazoned in the New York skyline
for more time than we had hoped
the failure of yesterday
the blindness of smoke

9/11

Looking up
a special effect
covered in ash
a sound
behind streaks
of titanium white

The sun he loved was hidden
behind an orange glow
no river
no Fourth of July

Shadows of powdered lovers
shuffle by
their eyes taped closed

He thought he heard her voice
under a siren's screech
saying she was fine
and this dark dream wants him to leave
we will find each other
within a cloudless peace

He could not see her ascension

He looked up
heaven was not out of the question
and the sky was filled with feathers

WHEN I HAVE SAID GOODBYE

When I have said goodbye
underground
dirt in my face
grit in my eyes

When my face has turned to stone
I will see
without flinching
what I have known

And God brings me around
never looking side to side
not believing
what I have been told

Soon I will not hear anything
except sweet kisses
on silent lips

WEEP WITH ME

Weep with me
Mother
Daughter
Friend
Hold on to me
Catch the tears as they stream
Steady the earth's shaking
Think of nothing but one loss
That will find itself
In the disappearance of life
And the emergence of hope
After the last eye has finished crying

FAIRY TALES

ATOMS SPEAKING

I hear the secret sounds
of atoms speaking
and see the universe
reshaping itself
while the elements
swirl and glow
and nothing is still

There is no evidence
of the silver towers
where thousands
once lived
embedded in fragments
that do not tell tales
of another existence

There is no molten rock to cool
she never asked you
to press your body against hers
with no hope of peace

THE MAGIC-MAKER

Everyone loves the magic-maker
he is wrapped around
the soul who knows
unbearable sweetness

Turning silk like flesh
into a Tour en l'air

And when the world is there
unclothed and written on his skin
we long to be the one who is in the air
the miracle that pulls you in

IN THE DARKNESS

In the darkness we fumble for forgiveness
for an hour we were perfect
and brought laughter to the masses
for an hour you were dashing
for a moment we were the same
as we had always been
then the hours became shorter
and the second loses time
and the nights do not remember who we are
and we would trade our peace of mind
for one normal minute in an agonizing day
when the night was still our friend
and let us crawl
under his lovely cover

MONET UNDERSTOOD

Monet understood
where morning, God and man
blended with the river
with its hint of ocean
and romantic love
painted with tinted air
always separate from the night
watching life begin
the river on the right
a sleeping barge
no one has told it to turn out the lights
their vigil is over

PLANTING FLOWERS

She did not think of planting flowers
her reflection had been stolen
ten years before
It was Halloween night
The ones who were supposed to love her
denied her loveliness
dipped her in blue
and tattooed the word 'whore'
over the tiny door
leading into her heart

DEAR WIND

Dear wind
dear mandolin
skim over the sparkle of letters written
glistening gray mosaic stone

Leave me there
when the tide is low
where I can hear the seagull sing
and hear the air

Leave me where the water rooms of sweetness
pull and push and glide
blanket me in evening tide

IN SHADOW

In shadow
I stood behind a body
that was as lovely
a memory as mine
I could not move
but for
the chant of clowns
I allowed my eyes
to be painted on
chiseled and chipped
it's harder to undo a life
made from stone

Someone looking very crisp
said it's a good English day to die

THE THREE WITCHES

The three witches
watched from the other room
my finest hour
stealing my perfect scenes
my perfect heart
stripped bare
unable to protect
how little was left
the battle is always to the finish
the border
the line
the last rite
the sharp end
or the ultimate unsure peace

DOORWAYS

Where the edge meets the door
where the lines of your life overlap
where love shatters glass
when a mother looks back
at the time that is too late
and hope crushes fate
when night becomes day
and the first light is last
when the die has been cast
it is too late to pray
you are walking through lines
joining ceilings and floors
and doorways meet doors

WHEREVER I LOOKED

Wherever I looked
she loomed
life's narrator
speechless orator
the demagination of my tragedy
sculpted in a primitive manner
pretending peace
while underneath
she caught things
too quick to see
within her sharpened beak

BUTTERFLY

She becomes a butterfly
Less useful
No longer speaking
No longer making anyone laugh
One season of color

She knows what she becomes

Drum beating on a chest
She imagines it is gone
Dropping wings on the water
On the unthinkable preserved man

His friends will know
Where he has been
And whom he has killed.

DHARMA

Words asleep
In my heart
For a hundred years

Dreams that speak in music
Of a life
Listening
To the slightest sound
In revelation

Your stories
Etched in glass
Over decades
Slowly, slowly

Where is the perfect line
I look for mine
She whispers and writes herself

Perfectly still
Between breaths

I wait for the page
That offers me the love
That I need to live
In return for filling up my spaces

EGGPLANT

When your mother goes
The place on earth
Reserved for you
Seems challenged

As she fought for your life
From before you were born
And made sure that you would eat
Eggplant, and never be hungry

Like Scarlett,
You'll never eat eggplant again
You vowed

So she helped to make you strong
And swore never to make your children
Eat eggplant either

And so this tale
Meant to be serious
Has turned a little funny
I guess it may have been the
Desire to stay away from the aubergine
That made you all this money.

HOW DARE THEY

I awaken to nightfall
Everyone is trying to steal my words
Images
Are mine, mine!

When left alone in my cave
God whispers a story
That only one can hear
Not two

So if you need to say that your thoughts
Are beautiful too
They are

But mine are like ripe little babies
Each with a life to live
and a history to create

While you've been criticizing everything and everyone
I've been in a place
Where learning to hear is the greatest gift

I watch the thoughts turn into angels
Standing guard, protecting me
From a stupid person
Who tells me that if they heed the time
They will go to my world
Where only I have the key

I AM A COLORED GIRL

I am a colored girl
Painted red
Outlined eyes
Faded beige curtains
Draped over heart-shaped dust
Of hardened alabaster

I am perfection
I own no past
Or airbrushed sheen
Mixed and matched

I am already here
I have not just arrived

I am the time worn fabric
Of freedoms face
I am the goal of it all
I am life's escape

I am not just born
I am too old
I am the firefly
Of my wisdoms soul

I am the calling
Of the setting sun
Asking hope to hurry
Asking me to be patient
And not look away
For this is where prayers are answered

WHO WAS I KIDDING

Who was I kidding
I was a raindrop
Far away from getting lost
In thought

I rule the world when it is raining
I lie on my cloud
Writing upside down
A raindrop waiting to disappear

It's morning and I am free
I can drink a diet coke
With caffeine if I please

When it is my time
My close family will say
She died of aluminum can poisoning
An overdose exacerbated
by her love of aspartame

SOLID AND FOREVER

I look at him who is a mystery
where does love begin?
the kind that cannot end
my eyes search for science to save me
I plead for the matter
that appears to move
to stand still
and call my love something
other than that
which is not solid and forever

He is like the air
this powerful swimmer
who glides to resist tides
that challenge the ocean
he is love you cannot see
and the illusion of something
you can touch

He is breath like me
the closest thing to forever
is a tremble of his voice
I reach for him in the air

*The following poems in this manuscript appeared in the November/December 2003 issue of *The American Poetry Review:*

Inhaling Lilacs **(published as #5)**
She Never Looked As Good After That **(published as #9)**
Ignorance **(published as #12)**
The End of Words **(published as #19)**
The Outline of My Body **(published as #24)**
Vanishing **(published as #27)**
No Ears, No Lies **(published as #32)**
Flesh **(published as #43)**

Edwards Brothers,Inc!
Thorofare, NJ 08086
13 April, 2011
BA2011103